C000112889

ROYAL NATIONAL
LIFEBOAT INSTITUTION **LIFEBOAT** SUPPORTED ENTIRELY BY
VOLUNTARY CONTRIBUTIONS

# up in the wind

## windmills

## Peter Ashley

ENGLISH HERITAGE

AN ENGLISH HERITAGE POCKET BOOK

*Up in the Wind* was Edward Thomas's first poem, written in 1914. There isn't a windmill in it because it's about a pub, but I found the title irresistible.

p 1 **Lytham St Anne's** LANCASHIRE
Lytham's seafront is a vast green space where children fly kites and men in panamas walk tiny dogs. The centrepiece is this fat Fylde mill snuggled up to the old Lifeboat Station.

p 2 **Chesterton** WARWICKSHIRE
See page 56

Published by English Heritage, Kemble Drive, Swindon SN2 2GZ
www.english-heritage.org.uk
English Heritage is the Government's statutory adviser on all aspects of the historic environment.

First published 2004

ISBN 1 85074 910 8

Product code 50964

*British Library Cataloguing in Publication data*
A CIP catalogue record for this book is available from the British Library.

Edited by Val Horsler
Page layout by Peter Ashley and Chuck Goodwin
Cover by Peter Ashley

Printed by Bath CPI

# contents

## introduction

*On a small green platform crowning a field of waving barley stands the windmill seen for miles around, the most picturesque feature in this sunny landscape, and to our delight is seen whirling round in its old-fashioned way, careless of the counter advantages of machinery and steam.*

*Poppy-Land*, Clement Scott

*To see a windmill's sails begin to turn at the bidding of a breath of wind imperceptible at ground level is to experience a moment of magic; it is an experience that can never pall.*

*Odd Aspects of England*, Garry Hogg

Windmills are amongst our most conspicuous landmarks, whether crowning a blowy hill-top, rising above village buildings, or isolated out on airy fenland. For the most part they were the workplace of dusty millers grinding the products of the surrounding fields but, in Eastern England, they could equally have been put to use as drainage mills, their sails turning giant scoop wheels that lifted water up from low-lying marshland and into rivers and drains.

We are first aware of them from their appearance in contemporary illustrated manuscripts in the 12th century. These were post mills, where the entire wooden superstructure, called a buck, pivoted on a stone base to face the wind. The 16th century saw the advent of the smock mill, usually an octagonal or even a twelve-sided weatherboarded building where only the cap carrying the sails rotated. Later the first tower mills of brick rose like lighthouses in the rural scene, monumental landmarks with numerous windows set in the often black-tarred or painted walls. So many of these are now jackdaw-haunted towers standing alone in the fields, gaunt shells where the wind funnels through empty window holes instead of turning the now vanished sails.

But there are memorable survivors where the unique silhouette of sails can still be seen set against the sky. Three windmills are preserved and maintained by English Heritage: the Saxtead Green Post Mill in Suffolk and the landmark tower mills at Sibsey in Lincolnshire and Berney Arms in Norfolk. On my travels I have also been overjoyed to find those mills that are once again producing flour.

The experience of a windmill rumbling with cogs and pulleys as giant millstones grind locally produced grain into characterful flours is one I cannot recommend highly enough – particularly as it has become part of the encouraging growing movement towards good local foods, made and sold locally. A really good reason to go out and buy a breadmaker.

This isn't a technical book, perhaps because I fear the wrath of those far more competent to talk about striking rods and lantern pinions. As with other titles in this series it's an introduction, looking at windmills as I found them in the landscape and, I hope, encouraging visits and flour-buying expeditions. Most of the mills featured here are easily accessible and are open to the public at least on a part-time basis. I've made it clear if they're private.

Windmills have a unique place in our consciousness; after all they were once the vital link between the corn in the fields and the basic ingredient for our bread. Or indeed all that stood between fenland drains and our tenuous hold on the land. They deserve our attention, but, more importantly, these beautiful eye-catchers deserve our respect for their original purpose.

# eastern england

### Berney Arms NORFOLK

This is English Heritage's most inaccessible property, so one of the most fun to get to. Your choices are limited to arriving either by boat (the mill stands near where the Rivers Yare and Waveney meet at Breydon Water) or by train to a tiny rose-strewn halt out on the green marshes. From the railway it's a short but atmospheric walk to the mill through long grass and reeds, where another person looming into sight in the heat looks like an apparition in an M R James ghost story.

## Berney Arms NORFOLK (continued)

Appearing like a mirage on a hot day, this is the tallest marsh mill in Broadland. It's been difficult to date precisely, but up in the cap someone has thoughtfully pencilled '1870'. She (mills are ladies, like ships) was very likely built to grind cement clinker, a by-product of cement formed from muddy deposits dredged up from the river bed. Clinker was also brought to the mill by wherry, for

a shilling a ton, from a steam cement plant at nearby Burgh Castle.

The latter years of her working life were taken up with draining the marshes, her sails turning the big scoop wheel housed in the weatherboarded casing called a hoodway. The paddles scooped water up from the lower level of the marsh and through a one-way iron hinged door into the upper level of the river.

At the time of my visit, the sails were separated from the cap by over a hundred miles, being restored at a millwrights in an Oxfordshire village near Henley-on-Thames.

## Horsey NORFOLK

Horsey Mere is the nearest broad to the coast, and a tiny channel branches off to the east with the Horsey Drainage Pump acting as a full stop at the end. It is in a state of excellent preservation, as you'd expect from the National Trust who have been its guardian since 1948. Originally built in the mid-19th century, it was extensively re-built in 1912 and 1987. It is good to see plain brickwork, with the white painted wooden mechanics making such a contrast. The internal machinery survives, but now the still very necessary pumping is carried out by a diesel engine.

## Waxham NORFOLK

Windmills are a favourite image to use in graphics, such is their immediately identifiable shape. A windmill has become the trademark for Broadland, and can be seen on everything from tea towels to petrol pumps. Here the Waxham Sands Holiday Park uses the Horsey Mill to great effect.

# Welcome to

## AM SANDS HOL

Tel 01692     5983

PERS     TOU

---

· SHOWERS · SHOP ·

ACH CAR

### Thurne NORFOLK

Windmills fulfil their landmark presence out on
Norfolk Broadland more than anywhere else.
Whilst walking down a hot lane near Ludham to
find St Benet's Abbey, I looked across the
countryside to see a white windmill against dark
trees about a mile away. The map revealed it to
be this exquisite 1820 drainage mill at Thurne, its
shape the result of a third storey being added to
the original two. By the time I arrived in the late
afternoon it had become a ghostly white moth
spreading its filigree wings by the River Bure, next
to holiday boats moored up for supper.

### St Benet's Abbey NORFOLK

Here first was an abbey, founded in c 800 but refounded by the Benedictines in 1019. It became supremely important and missed being demolished by the Dissolution, but by 1545 it was abandoned anyway. Little remains of this lonely abbey on the River Bure – just a few stones marked by a wooden cross cut from a Sandringham oak – but more of the gatehouse survives only because someone in the early 18th century used it as the support for a brick-towered windpump, probably the first mill of its kind in Norfolk. Its original purpose was as a drainage mill, but it may also have been used to extract oil for lamps from locally grown colza, which is more or less what we now know as rape seed.

## Sutton NORFOLK

The first mill arrived here in 1789, but suffered as many mills did from being burned down. The mill house of the same date survives, with fluted columns and a Doric porch, but this mill is the 1859 replacement. With nine floors and its Norfolk boat-shaped cap, this is one of Britain's tallest windmills, an awe-inspiring sight amongst the corn fields. There is something slightly other-worldly about it, and part of its immense charm for me is the patchwork of colour, the bricks showing through the weather-beaten white paint and the fading pink and blue carpentry. At its feet is the absorbing Broads Museum that displays just about everything from a 1912 milkman's tricycle to a packet of Passing Clouds cigarettes

### Cley-next-the-Sea NORFOLK

This windmill once featured in the BBC 1 channel identity that used an orange hot air balloon to represent the world arriving at the heart of a community. These wonderful pictures were of course scrapped to be replaced by images as meaningless as they are patronising, but the mill has more staying power and, apart from frequent film appearances, this is one of the most recognisable landmarks of the North Norfolk coast. Built in 1810, it worked at the centre of a port that only finally closed on the arrival of the railway at Holt in 1884. Cley Windmill carried on working for another 37 years.

### Burnham Overy NORFOLK

Anyone who has driven along the North Norfolk coast road will know of the tight double bend that twists past the red brick watermill that straddles the River Burn. The whole scene here is almost unspeakably picturesque: the mill with its overhanging weatherboarded hoist, the row of flint cottages, the narrow bridge and the Mill House with its wrought iron loggia. Looking out above it all is the windmill, erected in 1816 by Edward Savory to supplement his watermill operation. This often happened where business could justify it, but now the only machinery left is in the ogee cap. The rest of the six storeys are now a private house with sea views of Scolt Head and Holkham Bay.

### Denver NORFOLK

This mill with its ogee-shaped cap sits between the village and the great sluice gate on the Great Ouse. It was built in 1835 for John Parker, and from 1854 John Gleaves supplemented the wind power with a steam engine, itself superseded by a Blackstone oil engine. The last miller was Thomas Harris and milling came to a close in 1941 when one of the sails was struck by lightning. On Harris's death in 1969 his sister Edith gave the mill to Norfolk County Council, and it is now as busy with milling coach parties as it was grinding corn in its halcyon past.

### Great Bircham NORFOLK

An archetypal mill in a perfect setting. Great Bircham towers above the pantiled roofs of its ancillary buildings, a welcoming place with friendly people scurrying about amongst the flour sacks and warm loaves. This 1846 mill was derelict by the 1970s, but has been beautifully restored by John Lawn, complete with a new cap proudly topped with its finial. It is very rewarding to step onto one wooden floor to see the sails framed against the quiet countryside outside, and on to another to watch the fantail poised against the sky.

## Saxtead Green SUFFOLK

Perched on its roundhouse, the white-painted Saxtead Green Post Mill is a classic addition to the Suffolk landscape, standing in open country and still turning to face the wind next to fields of waving corn and the village green. Windmills tend to occupy the same site for generations, and indeed early records refer to a mill here in 1287. The present mill is first mentioned in 1796, and a succession of millers worked here producing flour until the First World War when, as with so many mills, it went over to grinding animal feed.

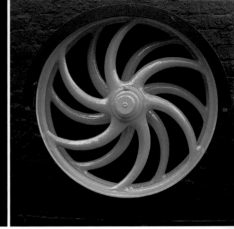

**Saxtead Green** SUFFOLK (continued)
The technical aspects of the machinery are thoroughly covered in the admirable English Heritage guide book written by that great windmill champion Rex Wailes, but very worthy of note here is the magnificent blue fantail, liable to move the entire mill at a moment's notice round its little railway track. The fantail was one of the first pieces of automatic machinery, only turning when the wind changes so that it moves the entire mill (buck), or in the case of a smock or tower mill just the cap and sails, into the wind.

∧ ⊓ **Aldeburgh** SUFFOLK

A heavily disguised mill at the southern end of Aldeburgh sea front. Judging by the coastal erosion that has left Aldeburgh's Moot Hall on the sea front instead of at the town centre, the chances are that this corn mill was at the heart of Slaughden, a lost village that once stood where the River Alde turns south to Orford. The private house that now incorporates the mill on Fort Green, with its green mill cap, pink shutters and fish weathervane, was designed by a Mr Briggs for a local parson and his Danish wife in 1902. It was described by Nikolaus Pevsner as a 'fantasia'.

> **Thorpeness** SUFFOLK

Thorpeness is one of very few purpose-built seaside resorts, a kind of Never Never Land as much for adults as children. Stuart Ogilvy began creating this remarkable adaptation of the garden suburb idea in 1910, when one of the water towers was disguised with a stage set house cloaking its tank 85 feet up the air, turning it into the magical House in the Clouds. The windmill at nearby Aldringham was uprooted, the corn-grinding machinery removed, and the weatherboarded edifice was slowly trundled to Thorpeness where it was perched on a new roundhouse with a pantiled roof . It was then put to work pumping water up to the House in the Clouds which stands on the other side of the sandy lane. The mill looks as if it could be the model for the front cover illustration for the Ladybird *Book of The Weather*.

### Great Bardfield ESSEX

This could be the oldest windmill in Essex, certainly one of the earliest to be converted into a home. Built in the mid-17th century it started its second term as a working mill in 1751, grinding corn right up to 1930. It may have started life as a wooden smock mill, but it is now encased in brick that was rendered over on its second conversion to a private house after the Second World War. The sails were lost in the great gales of October 1987, the present set being of the non-working variety. It is also known as 'Gibraltar' Mill.

∧ **Aythorpe Roding** ESSEX

The Rodings stretch out in lonely country between Harlow and Great Dunmow: Abbess, Aythorpe, Beauchamp, Berners, High, Leaden, Margaret and White. Roding rhymes with soothing. This 18th-century windmill at Gunners Green is the largest surviving post mill in Essex with four patent sails, steps attached to the fantail and two pairs of millstones. It is in full working order and open regularly during the summer.

> **Thaxted** ESSEX

There is much to enjoy in this corner of Essex. Down a path by the exquisite Chantry Almshouse is John Webb's tower windmill, built in 1804 with material from his own brickyard in the Chelmer Valley, and capitalising on the increasing need for milled products for a rapidly growing London population. The other Thaxted landmark seen here is the parish church, dedicated in triplicate to St John the Baptist, St Mary and St Laurence.

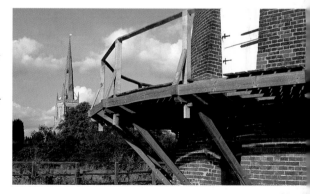

### Great Gransden CAMBRIDGESHIRE

Outside the village is a neatly-hedged square of lawn and this beautiful black weather-boarded post mill, restored by Thompsons of Alford in 1982–3. William Webb owned the mill in the 1860s, and it was in its dark recesses that he guiltily hid a book he had discovered amongst his deceased brother's effects. This was *The Infidel's Bible*, a witchcraft handbook, which of course meant that the mill stopped working immediately.

∧ **Bourn** CAMBRIDGESHIRE

The scale of Bourn Mill reminds me of those little post mills you see in medieval illuminated manuscripts, usually with a hooded peasant approaching it with an oversize sack on his back. It even has the typical flat-sided roof that so restricted room for the brake wheel; later English post mills had pointed-arch shaped roofs to allow freer movement around it. Surrey's Outwood Mill may be the oldest working post mill, but Bourn Mill claims to be the oldest surviving example, mention of it being made in documents of 1636.

**Madingley Mill** CAMBRIDGESHIRE
Just along the road from the American Military Cemetery, this mill was originally to be found in Ellington in Huntingdonshire. It was moved here in 1936, and an unexpectedly cheerful Pevsner describes it as having a 'petticoat covering the lower parts.'

### Heckington LINCOLNSHIRE

This mill is inseparable from the railway. Black-and-white steam era photographs of the station, on the Sleaford to Boston line, invariably have this unique eight-sailed windmill in the background. In 1830 the mill was built with only five sails, but after severe storm damage in 1890 the reconstruction by John Pocklington utilised the eight sails taken from Tuxford's Mill in Boston. The mill ceased to function after the Second World War, but in 1986 the sails turned again, and Heckington once more has stoneground flour milled on its doorstep. No other mill in the country has eight sails, and I always think it looks as if they're moving even when stationary, an illusion perhaps helped by the stabilising rods stretched between them.

### Boston LINCOLNSHIRE

Maud Foster is an enigmatic figure in the topography of Boston and the surrounding countryside. The slightly prim name is attached to a fenland drain, a sluice and this five-sailer tower mill of 1819. The lady in question was a 16th-century landowner who sold tracts of land for drainage, but the mill takes its name from the 1568 waterway on whose bank it stands. It was built by Hull millwrights Norman & Smithson, and restored to full working order in 1988. England's tallest working mill, Maud Foster mills flour all the year round.

### Alford LINCOLNSHIRE

Just where the Lincolnshire Wolds start to slope gently down to the green marshes and the sea is the unpretentious market town of Alford. In 1932 there were three windmills: a four-sailer, a five-sailer and a six-sailer. Only the five-sailer survives, a 72-feet-high tower mill built by local millwright Sam Oxley in 1837, a working mill capable of grinding nearly two tons of wheat a day in a strong wind. The interior is imbued with an atmosphere that combines the workmanlike practicalities of present-day milling with constant reminders of the past: a set of hoist chains rattling up and down next to hessian sacks printed with bold wooden type and fat flour bags imprinted with a drawing of the mill.

### Sibsey LINCOLNSHIRE

The Sibsey Trader Windmill stands out
in the flat Lincolnshire fields north of
Boston, an imposing tower mill built in
1877 by Saundersons of Louth. Its red
brick tower is tarred outside and
whitewashed inside, and – one of the few
surviving six-sailer mills – is now in the
care of English Heritage. The main sails
have shutters that open and close like
Venetian blinds to control the rotational
speed. They were manoeuvred by chains
operated by the miller from the second-
floor balcony. How like a sailing ship it
must have been, the miller as its captain
reefing his sails to best catch the wind
from the sea of fenland that stretches for
miles around.

**Sibsey** LINCOLNSHIRE (continued)
The tall tower windmill is almost the trademark for this part of England. Their passing in the latter half of the 19th century was the result of cheap American grain arriving at the East Coast ports, where it could be processed in the new steam mills and then distributed far beyond the immediate area by the railways.

> **Wainfleet All Saints** LINCOLNSHIRE

Wainfleet's tower mill is incorporated into Bateman's Brewery, a very fitting symbol for the potent mixing of barley and hops. A stylised version appears on their labels and the beer bottle weathervane swings in the wind above the castellated top that crowns what is a now a bar and the Bateman boardroom where the directors sit at a suitably round table. To para-phrase their motto, it's a good honest use for a retired windmill.

>> **Ellis' Mill** LINCOLN

A tower mill that plays hide and seek in the back streets of north Lincoln, standing on the edge of the Lincoln Cliff and looking across the plain to the River Trent. One gets a good view of it on the road coming in from Worksop, but close up it's invisible even when walking down Mill Road, until a gap in the red brick terraced houses reveals the tower standing above the roofs of bungalows below. An 1842 map reveals nine windmills in this area alone, and this remaining mill survived wartime ravages, and a huge fire in 1974, for a Civic Trust restoration to start in time to celebrate the Queen's Silver Jubilee in 1977.

## Kirton-in-Lindsey LINCOLNSHIRE

Mount Pleasant Mill is outside the village on the B1398 north towards Scunthorpe. Its history illustrates the changing fortunes of mills, from its arrival in 1875 to the present day when its four double-sided patent sails once more sweep the Lincolnshire sky. The Snell family worked the mill before selling it to Fred and Harry Banks in 1936, who removed the sails and installed a 20 hp Crossley oil engine. Throughout the 1950s and 1960s a fleet of Banks Brothers lorries departed and arrived in the yard until the mill was closed in 1973. It became idle and derelict until restoration, including new sails by Thompson's of Alford, resulted in the fully operational mill reopening in 1991.

A pair of cast-iron governors compensate for varying wind speeds, automatically regulating the gap between the millstones to give consistency of pressure.

### Moulton LINCOLNSHIRE

Nikolaus Pevsner reckoned this was the tallest mill in the country and looked like a giraffe. With its corrugated iron cap I think it's more like an elephant's trunk balancing a fairy cake in its frilly paper case, but its claim as the tallest may well be realised soon with the replacement of the sails. They came off in 1895 in what is a miller's worst nightmare – when, after relatively calm weather, a gale blew up in the opposite direction from the previous wind. The crashing noise of the storm battering the wrong side of the sails woke the miller who rushed out to try and turn the cap so that the sails faced the onslaught, but it was too late. It was the end of the wind generation for this mill, which was then powered by steam, diesel and finally electricity.

Inside is a cornucopia of detail: a little sunlit office with an Imperial typewriter on a desk well-rubbed with the passage of time, and sacks with the miller's name, Biggadike, attached to the end of a well-used wooden chute.

# western england

### Wilton WILTSHIRE

Windmills are a rarity in the south west, and here in Wilton is the last surviving working windmill in Wiltshire. This should be watermill country, but the building of the Kennet and Avon Canal took away the precious waters of the River Bedwyn that supplied several mills in the locality. And so this mill took their place in 1821, a five-floor brick tower with unusual round-headed windows. Steam and electric power, as at so many mills, provided more consistent energy for milling, and Wilton Mill went into decline in the 1920s. But good sense triumphed once again, and 80 years later the mill is once again producing flour.

## Wedmore SOMERSET

The 18th-century Ashton Mill was the last windmill to grind corn in Somerset. It has a vaguely continental look with its 23-ft-high cylindrical tower topped out with its wooden boat-shaped cap which, like the one at Stembridge, would have originally been thatched. The advantageous position above the Somerset Levels that gave the mill its wind was also recognised in wartime when it was used as a look-out post for the Home Guard.

## Swindon WILTSHIRE

On the interminable ring roads of Swindon there is a sign pointing to the Windmill Hill Business Park. This pale-bricked tower mill stands amongst all the e-mails and mouse mats, and was brought here in the mid-1980s from Chiseldon on the other side of the M4 to be the centre piece of the new commercial venture.

## High Ham SOMERSET

Stembridge Windmill is probably the last remaining thatched mill in the country. There may be others, but none is as complete as this one. There is a slightly fey appearance to it, something of the dark fairy story where the miller could easily be an anthro-pomorphic fox or badger. It arrived here in this remote part of Somerset in 1822, built in the roughly coursed local lias stone with the thatch covering a weatherboarded gable. Steam power brought the sails to rest in 1897, but now it's a star in the National Trust catalogue.

# central england

## Brill BUCKINGHAMSHIRE

Brill is a hilltop village in lonely country between Bicester and Thame. Although in Buckinghamshire, the panoramic view southwards is of a patchwork of Oxfordshire fields diminishing away towards the Thames Valley. The post mill stands in isolation from any other buildings, the classic story book position. Around its base are steep-sided hollows where clay was extracted for bricks and tiles, and medieval kilns have been found on the common. It is now a glorious playground where children play hide-and-seek and fly their kites. The mill itself is 600 feet above sea level, built here in 1680, although the brick roundhouse with its shingle roof was rebuilt in 1948. It last milled barley in 1919, and was once capable of producing 180lbs of flour in an hour.

## Chesterton WARWICKSHIRE

The Fosse Way is a Roman road cutting across the grain of England from Dorset to Lincolnshire. About half way along its length a curious sight appears, just above the road in a remote corner of Warwickshire. This elephantine windmill looks out over the lost estate of Sir Edward Peto, whose 17th-century house was demolished in 1802. Peto is most likely to have been the designer of what was originally a 1632 observatory, although it is often attributed to Inigo Jones. A small room sits on six circular arches, and the sails were once able to face the wind by revolving with the leaden domed roof. Up until the 1930s the local point-to-point races were watched from this eyecatching grandstand amongst the thistles of Windmill Hill.

### < **Napton-on-the-Hill** WARWICKSHIRE

I include this privately-owned windmill purely
because of its position, a landmark for all those
who have navigated the Oxford Canal as it rounds
Napton Hill near Southam in Warwickshire. In his
book *Narrow Boat* L T C Rolt recalls mooring under
it: *A derelict tower mill...crowns the hill, looking across
to its fellow at Burton Dassett, and the canal curved
so closely beneath the slope that our moorings were
almost in the shadow of the gaunt sails.*

### > **Kibworth Harcourt** LEICESTERSHIRE

Probably built in the early 17th century, this post
mill hides behind trees in a farmyard. It was last
used for its proper purpose in the 1920s, the
entire structure turning on just a single tree trunk,
independent from the brick walling added much
later to act as a storage area. There is no public
access to the mill, but it was once a favourite
meeting place for the local Fernie Hunt.

## Whissendine RUTLAND

This beautiful honey-coloured mill looks out over cow pastures in quiet Rutland countryside. One's arrival here is greeted by the deep rumblings of the mill's machinery and the welcoming presence of a truly dusty miller. It was built in 1809 by the nearby Stapleford Estate who sold it in 1862. The sails stopped turning on the 20th April 1922, the last journeyman miller rejoicing in the name of Horace Augustus Hallet. But once again it vibrates with life, with so much to fire the imagination. The arrival of big cotton sacks of grain from local farms, the spinning of the magnificent spur wheel driving rattling canvas belts, rarities like the Patent Wegmann roller, and the pencil scribblings of generations of millers that could have been written yesterday.

∧ **Ketton** RUTLAND

This lonely stone-rendered mill sits above the limestone village of Ketton, an owl-haunted shell with its back to woods where two 4ft-diameter French millstones were discovered. Nigel Moon of Whissendine, in his definitive *Leicestershire and Rutland Windmills,* thinks that its demise was possibly hastened by the competition offered by a new steam mill across at Luffenham, and by 1904 the Ordnance Survey map was already marking it as an 'Old Windmill'.

< **South Luffenham** RUTLAND

This empty tower stands alone out in the stubble of a Rutland field, the wide spaces around it emphasing its scale in a way denied to many derelict tower mills surrounded by trees or ancillary buildings and cottages. Above the door is a stone plaque with the date 1832, and an advertisement inviting tenders for its erection was placed in June of the same year. New Year's day in 1900 saw another advertisement appear offering for sale the surviving pieces of the mill's machinery.

### Green's Mill NOTTINGHAM

The village of Sneinton is now totally absorbed into the city of Nottingham, but its windmill still crowns the ridge overlooking the valley of the River Trent. The brick tower with its 'ogee' or onion dome was built by George Green in 1807 and worked for over 60 years producing flour for the city's bakeries and animal feed for the immense population of horses. The miller's son, George Green Junior, managed to be not only a successful miller but also one of the foremost scientists of the 19th century. His theories on electricity, magnetism, light and sound were based on a system of mathematics that is still used the world over. Restoration completed in 1986 means that flour is once again ground and weighed out in Mr Green's mill.

### Outwood SURREY

Outwood is the ultimate calendar pin-up mill, but it's also in the windmill hall of fame as Britain's oldest working mill, having stood up here on a Surrey common since 1665. It is a fascinating thought that this mill was being built as the Great Plague raged in London, less than 25 miles away, and that in the following year the glow of the Great Fire was seen from its upper storey. Outwood is a post mill, where the whole body of the mill turns to face the wind, rotating on top of a roundhouse. To turn the mill, the stairs must first be raised and then the massive tailpole put to work in moving the buck to face the wind. The whole thing is so finely balanced that one person can do it. The stairs are then let down again, acting as an anchor and stabiliser for the mill. Outwood is privately owned, but is regularly open to the public.

### Wimbledon GREATER LONDON

Anyone who has stopped for tea in the middle of Wimbledon Common will know
this windmill perched on its yellow brick octagonal base. It was designed by carpenter
Charles March in 1817, an uncommon composite type that was formerly a hollow
post mill with a vertical shaft that drove machinery in the roundhouse below. Its
working life was less than 50 years, when the roundhouse was enclosed in stock
London brick and divided up into six cottages. The most appealing feature for me is
the white-painted timber balustrading and the series of bright orange chimney stacks.

## Sarre KENT

Built in 1820 by the prolific millwright John Holman of Canterbury, this smock mill was heightened by nine feet in 1854 by jacking up the whole structure on to a rebuilt brick base. (The term 'smock' comes from the resemblance of this type of mill to a 19th-century countryman's overall that flared out from the neck.) Like so many mills, Sarre fell into decay as its usefulness finished. But once again the dedication of those who love these things triumphed over the odds, and the mill is not only restored to full working order but is also once again producing high-quality stoneground flour. There is something very satisfying about being able to buy (and eat) a loaf or a bun that is made from flour ground just feet away, as a scarecrow keeps a very beady eye out for the next delivery of grain.

**Margate** KENT

Drapers is a c1845 smock mill built by John Holman of Canterbury, and contains many fascinating glimpses of the agricultural past, with a little museum showing carpenters' and joiners' tools, weights and measures and farm implements. My favourite is this beautiful Bamford's Patent Rapid Mill No 20, a product of the same Uttoxeter company that later produced the world-famous JCB. On this sunny Sunday afternoon there was also something headily romantic about the big hollyhocks nodding slowly against the hot tarred wood.

### Halnaker WEST SUSSEX

Halnaker is reached by climbing a lane overhung with trees, cutting up through the chalk above Chichester. The shady track opens out onto a steeply-rising open field to where the tile-hung brick tower waits at the summit. It was built here for the Goodwood Estates in 1750, but is now only an empty shell, restored as a memorial to the wife of Sir William Bird. It inspired Hillaire Belloc to write his eponymous poem in 1912: *'And the sweeps have fallen from Ha'naker Mill. Ha'naker Mill is in desolation: Ruin a-top and a field unploughed.'*

### Shipley WEST SUSSEX

Here is the largest smock mill in Sussex. The millwright, believe it or not, was a Mr Grist and it goes under a number of names: King's Mill, Belloc's Mill, Vincent's Mill and the one I like best, Mrs Shipley. Hillaire Belloc lived nearby from 1906 when he purchased a house and the 1879 mill. The mill sails turned again after the 1958 restoration was completed in his memory, noted on a plaque:
*Let this be a memorial to Hillaire Belloc who garnered a harvest of wisdom and sympathy for young and old.*

### Clayton EAST SUSSEX

Jack and Jill are two mills in close company up on a chalk track across the South Downs, with views as far afield as the North Downs and the Ashdown Forest.

> Jack is so obviously the lad, a privately-owned black-tarred bruiser of 100,000 bricks glowering behind the hedge.

∧ Jill is the white weatherboarded post mill sitting demurely a little lower down the hill. They both look down over the villages of Ditchling and Hassocks and in between them, amazingly, are the remains of a third mill called Duncton, built in 1774.

**West Blatchington** BRIGHTON & HOVE

This curious mill is up on a hill above the teeming seaside resort of Brighton. Now surrounded by suburban houses in a quiet backwater, this weatherboarded smock mill perches on top of a barn built of the local flinty chalk. It stood at the heart of a downland farmyard that has now metamorphosed into a carefully-mown traffic island. The sails first turned in 1820, but 80 years later they finally ceased to grind corn. Much of the original machinery survives in a little museum in the barn together with items rescued from other Sussex mills.

### Nutley EAST SUSSEX

Away in woodland at the edge of the
Ashdown Forest is this wonderfully
evocative post mill. We first discovered it
on a cold and windy Easter Monday,
following a sign that pointed down a
path through gorse bushes from the
Forest to where we got very excited at
seeing the sails moving round behind the
trees. It was open, so we all clambered
up into its dark timber recesses, the faces
of the children looking around in awe
and apprehension as the whole mill
shook and tumbled in the wind. It was
first recorded in 1840 when Henry
Selford ground corn for local
smallholders, but it was very likely moved
(as mills often were) from either
Crowborough or Goudhurst in Kent.

# THE DAWN OF A NEW ERA

## HOLLAND'S
### SELF-RAISING FLOUR

EMPIRE BUYING BEGINS AT HOME

Copyright

Registered No. 1832

**YOUR GUARANTEE OF PURITY**

Made and Packed by

## A·J·HOLLAND LTD

from the Finest Wheat in East Anglia.

## Audley End Station, ESSEX.

# 3 LB. NET.

## acknowledgements

I would like to thank the mill owners and keepers who were welcoming and helpful to me in my quest: in particular: Nigel Moon at Whissendine, Geoff Dees and Claudia Kirk at Alford Mill, Marie-Christine Austin at Mount Pleasant Windmill, Sheila Thomas at Outwood Mill, Ken Lidbetter at Ellis' Mill, Lincoln, and David Briggs at Kibworth Harcourt. Thanks also to: Val Horsler and Rob Richardson at English Heritage, John Storey in Aldeburgh, Bateman's Brewery, Larry Flynn, Margaret Shepherd for milling around Kent with me, Lucy Bland, David Stanhope, Gee and Rupert Farnsworth, Chuck Goodwin and Biff Raven-Hill.

## bibliography

*Windmills in England*, Rex Wailes, The Architectural Press, 1948

*Windmills*, Suzanne Beedell, David & Charles, 1975

*Leicestershire and Rutland Windmills*, Nigel Moon, Sycamore Press 1981

*Buildings of England Series*, Penguin, Yale University Press

*The Great Level*, Dorothy Summers, David & Charles, 1976

*The Fenland*, Anthony Parker & Denis Pye, David & Charles, 1976

*Odd Aspects of England*, Garry Hogg, David & Charles, 1968

*East Anglia & The Fens*, Rob Talbot and Robin Whiteman, Weidenfeld & Nicolson 1996

Clement Scott's *Poppy-Land*, quoted in the introduction, was a collection of his *Daily Telegraph* writings about his excursions in the 1880s to the area around Cromer in Norfolk. He stayed in the Mill House, next to the windmill in Sidestrand, and his musings made celebrities of the miller, Alfred Jermy, and his daughter Louie. *Poppy-Land* is now available in a delightful facsimile edition published by Christine Stockwell.

< Your guarantee of purity from an Essex miller, a flour bag label with a proper weight measurement.

*Overleaf:*
**Ashton Mill** WEDMORE SOMERSET